Minimalism

Methods For Streamlining Your Life And Arranging Your Living Space, Including Engaging Tasks And Physical Training

(Minimalist Bakery's Book Of Minimalism A Mind-set Of Minimalism Living Simply Ways To Reduce Expenses)

Glória Pereira

TABLE OF CONTNET

Pieces Of Furniture 1

The Liberty That You Obtain 9

Identifying Your "Why" 23

Getting Ideas From Recognized Personalities 42

Organising The House 58

Lism Has The Power To Improve Your Life 77

Examine Your Various Relationships In Your Life . 95

How To Turn Down Free Things 113

Sustaining Optimal Health 126

How A Minimalist Lifestyle Can Improve Your Quality Of Life 143

Pieces Of Furniture

Consider how much of your lounge's furnishings are essential. This will depend on the size of your family, the frequency and quantity of visitors, and the style of furniture you choose. If you interact frequently, you should have enough space for everyone in the family to sit or go for the gold plus additional guests. Some people never hide anything from you, furniture that is hardly touched. People are occasionally convinced to purchase "sets" of furniture that are either unnecessary or, in the end, too large for their rooms. Think about what you need and require. If you are a parent, it may be wise to forgo purchasing an expensive lounge chair that your children will likely use for a long time. The same is true for animals, who usually identify their #1 spot on the furniture, even if it goes against your values.

The idea is to increase comfort for every family member without sacrificing quality or overspending. Some people treat their apartments like historical sites, losing their cool when their expensive furniture falls apart. For most things and everyone, crumbling is a normal part of living. If you never enjoy a pricey furniture set to the fullest, what good is it?

Stretched-out furniture makes room for bookracks, shelves, cabinets, stands, and other large, potentially difficult-to-move items. If any of these are essential to have around, consider them and take steps to make them more useful or take them out of play. We will go over a lot to help restrict what is stored in these places.

On TV:

During my journey of moderation, I realized how absurd it is for the TV to be the central point of convergence for an entire family room. The main thing we noticed was that it was in the exact location as the TV was going, regardless of where I moved or when I assisted others in transferring. Is this case really that important to our reality? So crucial that we address its circumstances first and then figure out how to accommodate everything else? You could answer "yes," "no," or "somewhere in the middle" to this question. It's your decision, and ideally, you weigh the advantages and disadvantages of having your TV serve as the focal point of your living area.

Many people have given up watching TV to focus on the things that matter more daily. Gone are the countless hours that passed while watching TV shows that did little more than serve as a distraction. The enormous sums of money spent on the TVs are no longer necessary, but the services provided to make the images appear on the screen are. Goodbye to the notion that "bigger is better," Let's keep our TV as big as possible. You can now use these hours and money on hobbies, people who are important to you, or anything else you can think of to do with the savings.

Although it might seem easy to argue against TV, there are certain benefits. Some TV shows offer excellent learning opportunities or can unite families and foster a mutual appreciation of programs. The idea is to choose these priceless opportunities carefully. Is it wise for you to hold onto your TV? Make every effort to only spend mulittlebittime in front of the TV unleift is how you define moderation. See if you can use the radio instead of the TV. It's enjoyable to replace TV with radio since you can listen to so much free entertainment from around the globe, and your brain organizes the events rather than a screen. These days, finding information that you would enjoy is easy, thanks to mobile phones and other innovations.

If you decide to keep your television on, please consider the following to save money and time. Could your phone replace your TV with what you see with your PC or mobile device? Do you have to provide a TV-specialized company with large quantities of money? Think to yourself how many of the available channels you watch. Is there a more affordable package you could use or a web-based tool that could save you a significant amount of money for a small monthly fee? If all you watch on TV is your local stations, consider getting an HDTV radio wire. These are not the "hare ears" of the past, albeit some are tiny, smooth receiving wires installed on nearby stations without a purpose. Yes, you may be paying a company to provide you with something you might obtain for free. There are moments when the free HDTV radio signal quality is better than the paid version.

I would be happy to provide information about my preferences if you have any questions about the services above. I've spent a lot of time and effort cutting down on my TV watching and similar activities, and I also like helping others save money in these areas.

The Liberty That You Obtain

When you practice minimalism to its fullest, you cut back on things that cause you to feel depressed or hopeless about life. How frequently do you turn on the television but never actually watch it? How many times have you claimed to be busy all day long when, in reality, all you did was clean your house and take out your trash? Now that you've emancipated yourself from that boredom, you may appreciate your independence more and stop letting your stuff rule your life. Your house will look better. After a week at work, your mind will be free to relax at home, and you won't have to fear returning to a disorganized home.

With this freedom, you can extend your living space outside by opening your doors to the backyard and adding garden furniture. Alternatively, you can use nature's benefits indoors by going outside. Because you cut ties with those who only desired a take-take connection and surrounded yourself with the positivity that propels joyful lives, you can spend more time with your family and true friends.

You could even wish to pick up a new pastime to pass the time. I never looked back after I started playing an instrument. I know people who have taken up this lifestyle, and they have taken more trips and picked up new languages. It is possible to improve your life without relying on material belongings. These days, television, phones, and the Internet have a huge impact on us, and the invasion of our privacy is so extreme that it causes tension and depression in many individuals. Releasing yourself from consumerism allows you to recognize your priorities and the everyday worth of your life. Because you are who you choose to be, you are free from the bonds of social expectations, but it doesn't mean you aren't connected to anyone. Since they believed minimalism offered a genuine escape from the life of servitude they were leading, most of my close friends had chosen to follow my example.

You have an option. It all begins with the mindset. When you have a mindset that keeps you in the present, you will also discover that you are happier and more at peace with yourself, that you form more meaningful friendships, and that you have more to offer the world because you have freed yourself from the belief that having more possessions makes your life more valuable. It's not, and once you realize how wonderful it is to know that less really is more, you won't likely go back to your previous habits. I have two options because anything I purchase substitutes something else. What I'll purchase and discard to adhere to my minimalist principles.

Chapter 4: Practical Advice for the Minimalist

Even if leading a moderate lifestyle is associated with purging rather than organizing, the association still has a role. When beginning the adventure, there are a few tricks and tips to keep in mind, along with some fascinating things to discover as you explore every section of the new street you have chosen to explore.

While cleaning, there are a few things to keep in mind. If that's the case, you might need to get a container for your scattered papers. Besides, not everything needs to be purchased to be resolved. Some people get planners for their storage rooms because they come with twenty gorgeous, distinctive towels. Are you going to need twenty?

It's also important to remember to give up on deal searching. For some, the thrill of discovering an amazing bargain is just as astounding as the purchasing instinct. You might be able to buy what you truly want when you truly want it and avoid having to haggle over price. This suggests that you won't fill your life with unnecessary possessions and that the ones you acquire will be of the highest caliber, lasting a long time.

Additionally, you won't be financially constrained by the more expensive cost because you have saved money by continuing to lead a moderate lifestyle.

Use the time you have wisely. You have more time now that you've rid yourself of unnecessary possessions. Since you're not rebuilding or cleaning them, use that time to complete something worthwhile.

Start small if you have a lot of stuff and are unsure where to start. Maintaining a modest lifestyle should release you from pressure. Therefore, beginning the cycle shouldn't make you feel any more anxious. Whether starting small entails managing a corner at a time or not, there is still more progress than you have made in months or even years.

Try to visualize that item in your life in a year if you are having trouble deciding whether it deserves a place in your moderate style of living. Don't purchase it at that moment if you cannot see it. The focus of minimalism is "presently." This is the perfect time to do it; this is the perfect time to take control of your life; this is the perfect time to set boundaries and live simply. If you come across something in your house that you've grown to believe is useless, take it immediately and use it to accomplish something; you can either discard it in the garbage or store it in a "gift" container in your garage.

"Will it fit in a cupboard?" is a question you should ask yourself when organizing and cleaning your kitchen. If not, consider how frequently you use it. Should you not have used it more than once in the preceding month, get rid of it. If you have used it but people often comment on its size, try putting it up for auction or giving it away and acquiring something smaller. Eating what you need is what moderation means: not abstaining from consumption.

Remain steady at all times when cleaning up. You will need to put in some mental work to change your lifestyle because you have lived a consumerist lifestyle for so long. The new mess will follow you for a long time, so be on the lookout for when it begins to come together. Then, take all necessary steps to thoroughly clean up. In the end, moderation will become the new normal in your life, and chaos will perceive you as less and less.

If you purchase something fresh and unique, replace it with something from the past. Assuming you purchased a better seat, you don't need to grip that unsteady one.

Enhancing your life is another aspect of minimalism, in addition to what you never keep. Instead of spending money on goods and products, use the money saved to pay for experiences and services that will ultimately improve your life. Possess a sense of daring? Try skydiving indoors! Enjoy taking trips? Spend a weekend traveling to a different part of the nation just to experience it! These activities will give you life-enhancing experiences that help you develop as a person rather than add more chaos.

Some people see a huge variable when cleaning up a home association. Not only do many people have a mess, but their mess is a direct result of their carelessness. Therefore, we've also included a few pointers on how to stay organized most effectively. Create a well-rounded foundation for something first. When your mail arrives, a balancing board with small boxes or bushels is a good place to start. Sort your incoming mail into one box and your outgoing mail into another. Work on this gentle movement until it becomes a habit, and then use it to improve another area of your life.

For most people, being disorganized is not having any authoritarian routines.

Give up juggling many projects at once. Those who experience disruptions may do so periodically because they always try to do everything simultaneously. Maybe it's a direct result of poor time management skills, but the most important thing anyone can do to address this problem causing disruption is to stop juggling multiple tasks. Once you start something, don't stop working on it until it's finished or you've reached your daily goal. It will not be easy immediately, but it will become second nature if you put in the effort.

Simplifying your financial situation is another way to become more organized.

If your responsibilities and payments are always piling up, it can get overwhelming, and you can forget about your expenses. If you have money in the hands of a reliable person, consider settling your debt by transferring your required payments to the bank. After that, configure scheduled charges using your data. You should do this for all of your payments since you can do this by going in and creating a recurring alert on your phone that will run every month without having to set a termination date once you have established a regular date and time for the auto-charge installment. Simple, Tested Steps to Clear Your Life and Enjoy the Benefits That Trickle Down

As we've seen, living a completely Zen and mindful life begins with decluttering. Clutter might act as an obstacle to achieving your desired life, as we have already observed. It's difficult to picture the life you want when surrounded by clutter, which confines you to what you can see right now. In what way? You become frustrated and disappointed in yourself when you surround yourself with constant clutter that serves as a constant reminder of the life you are not living and the one you ought to be living.

Decluttering is a surefire way to improve your life, pursue your objectives, and finish tasks. By decluttering, you can let go of everything, including feelings impeding your success. Decluttering is a process, as I've already mentioned, especially if it's done for serenity and well-being. It requires time. Here are some pointers to get you going.

Identifying Your "Why"

I have mentioned this in passing. Determine your motivation before you start the decluttering process. Why is decluttering your life and house necessary? What else motivates the desire besides the obvious truth that you ought to? The greatest way to declutter is to link it to a personal objective. Use this to your advantage, for instance, if your objective is to maintain organization or generate income through saving. Your motivation for decluttering is its fuel. You can envision your life after successfully decluttering if you decide on it in advance (before starting the process). Anything might be your "why." You may even want to use your garage or locate something right away in the morning. You'll be halfway there once you figure out why. Ultimately, a thousand miles begin with a single step.

You need to address a second reason besides the one you have for wanting to declutter. What makes you "collect"? Three types of people tend to have cluttered personalities in general:

#The Storekeeper - The storekeeper keeps items in storage because they believe they might be useful.

#The romantic: The romantic is sentimental and holds onto things.

#The Pollyana - Stores mismatched items in the expectation that they will eventually be fixed to match.

Each of the three groups has a unique decluttering strategy. If you own a store, dispose of, or sell anything you haven't used in at least six months (give yourself a deadline). If you identify as a romantic, please respond. "Does the relationship or emotion strengthen when you hold the item?" "Will your emotions fade or disappear if the item disappears?" Conversely, Pollyanna ought to establish a schedule for every revitalization effort. Give it away or discard it if your item has not been matched after a certain amount of time.

Determine

Not all of your possessions are cluttered. There are a few jewels to preserve hidden behind the mess. What leaves and what stays must be decided. This is the enjoyable portion. Take a large box or two and store all of your kitchen utensils inside of it (make sure it is clean) to declutter your space. Remove items from their boxes and return them to their designated kitchen racks or areas after use. Anything left in the box after two months of this is clutter. Give it away or sell it. *Turn every article of clothes inside out and place it on its hanger in your closet. Every time you wear anything, make sure to hang it properly after cleaning it. Three months later, assess your development. * Anything that is still hanging inside out during that time expires. Focus on the primary purpose of the living room. Do you watch films on it or do you use it for relaxation? Keep pertinent stuff in this area once you decide how to use the space. For instance, store books and videos in this area if you plan to watch movies or read for pleasure in this room. This does not imply that you hold onto your old Nintendo game when you no longer play it or own the system. Please give away any games or books you are not using. Regarding the loo: Take any medications you haven't taken in a few months out of your medicine cabinet. Get rid of any old, dried-up makeup from your ideal area. You may also apply the box approach we used in the kitchen for the bathroom.

deciding on a "staging" location

You can store everything you get rid of in a staging area until you sell or donate it. Most people err by selecting a staging spot that is out of sight. This is incorrect. As you enter and exit your house, choose a spot for your staging area. This ensures that you never forget to act on the item or items. If you are selling or giving things away, it also guarantees that you can track the movement of everything leaving your house.

Commence distributing or marketing.

Contact a charity if you have chosen to donate the items on your purge list. The majority of charities will gladly make arrangements for pickup. To generate some quick cash and maintain the selling momentum, begin with the objects you think are valuable if you decide to sell them. This is very helpful, in my experience, if you want to save money. Use a portion of the sale's earnings, whatever your objective, to achieve it.

PART 4: THE ADVANTAGES OF MINIMALISM FOR YOUR FINANCES

1. LESS AREA IS REQUIRED:

This translates to lowering your rent or mortgage payment: You don't need as much room to store everything you've gathered when you practice minimalism. Buying or renting a smaller property can help you save money on rent while allowing you to have a beautiful, modern house you adore. You might find that cutting back will save you money after you start to get rid of some of your possessions. It will enable you to spend more money on the things that are truly essential to you by saving you money on utilities, rent, and other expenditures.

2. ALLOWS YOU TO MANAGE YOUR SPENDING: Living a minimalist lifestyle forces one to concentrate on the things that are most important to them. It will,

of course, have an impact on your financial decisions. Focusing on certain experiences rather than specific things will shift your spending habits. Having a clear understanding of your priorities will help you make spending plans, which can subsequently influence how you handle money in general.

Debt-free: One way to streamline your money is to pay off your debt.

Many people use their credit cards exclusively for emergencies after fully paying off their credit card debt. Paying off debt makes life much easier. It lets you take a year off to travel or quit a job you don't enjoy.

4. MINIMALISM REDUCES THE NEED FOR STUFF: A common aspect of

minimalism is reducing the amount of stuff you own.

If you truly need to make significant expenditure cuts, it can help you save money or pay off debt because you own fewer items and spend less on purchases. As a result of your reduced purchases, you will have more money to allocate to other financial objectives and can shift your attention from material possessions to experiences.

5. HELP YOU TO DEFINE YOUR CASH FLOW: You can do several things to simplify the process of managing your money. On the same day, you can pay off all of your bills. For normal transactions, you can switch to cash, which makes tracking your spending simpler.

Additionally, you might wish to search for software or an application that simplifies financial administration.

6. ASSISTS YOU IN MAINTAINING YOUR FISCAL PLANNING AND GOALS:

Being mindful of your surroundings is key to minimalism. It can support you in setting and achieving financial goals. Making a spending plan based on your current priorities is known as budgeting. Determining what matters most to you makes it easier to decide how and when to spend your money.

It can also help you determine which aspects of your money management, such as the interest rate you pay each month on different loans, require adjustments.

Place a mesh sports hammock with balls and other small stuff inside as a work area.

Attics and Basements

Items shouldn't be kept on the basement floor. Construct wall-to-wall shelves and store objects in plastic containers. Assign each person a specific area in the basement or attic to store stuff, and mark what belongs there.

Stow seasonal or infrequently used goods to the rear or bottom of the storage rooms and arrange often used items in the most accessible places.

You can hang things from walls or ceilings.

Makeover and Organise Your Car

This is how you can thoroughly clean and disinfect your car to take a step towards achieving a modest standard of living.

Clean: Start by getting rid of all the trash. Proceed progressively towards the rear of the vehicle after starting at the front. Only objects that belong in the car should be kept; anything else should be thrown out or taken from the house or garage.

Wipes: Use wipes to clean the dashboards, armrests, and steering wheel.

Floor mats: Shake off any dust by removing the floor mats. Next, hoover.

To eliminate smells, apply baking soda and hoover the next morning.

Door pockets: Take out the empty wrappers and plastic bottles from the door pockets.

Glove compartment: Although people frequently overpack the glove compartment, only a few necessities should be kept inside, such as:
Pen and a tiny notepad
Owner's manual for a vehicle
log of vehicle maintenance
Information about roadside assistance
Evidence of registration and insurance
a compact first-aid kit
tire pressure gauge

Visor: You may conveniently store recipes, phones, or sunglasses with an organizer fastened to the driver's or passenger's side visor. Cup holders: To keep the cup holders from getting sticky, insert a few silicone cupcake liners inside of them.

Back seats: Toys, apparel items, and food wrappers all contribute to the mess in the back of the vehicle. Use the front seat's rear portion as a hanging organizer to keep games, books, or other items. Shoe organizers work well for holding food and toys because of their perfectly sized compartments.

Boot: A first aid kit or other necessities are ideal for storage in the boot.

Cleaning the mess will help you organize your car, save time, and reduce driving miles.

Reduce the Size of Your Office

Your workspace must be designed to complement your balanced lifestyle. Here's how to go about it:

Put Your Desk in Order

Label your file system and boxes appropriately so that others can find critical documents quickly while you are away.

Make your tasks a priority and complete them one at a time. Putting off work is one of the biggest causes of clutter on desks. Tasks accumulate, resulting in missed deadlines and wasted time.

Start immediately working on a pass, trash, or act mentality. Every paper that lands on your desk should be examined. Is this document urgent? Or is it just junk mail or something already on your computer? Get rid of paperwork you don't need, give documents to the appropriate parties, and take urgent action on issues.

Assign a spot to the things you plan to bring home. Items like your keys, phone, wallet, personal paperwork, read-aloud articles, briefcase, or purse shouldn't be kept on the desk.

Having one or two images on your desk is a good idea. They inspire you to work and remind you of the reasons behind your daily commute to and from the office.

Clear off clutter from your work PC and set up a simple file structure. Both you and other users of your work computers will benefit from this.

Put filing cabinets in order. Always place objects in their correct locations and use hanging file folders with labels. This will facilitate finding information more quickly. Sort your files correctly and store important papers, such as financial and warranty information, on different file systems.

Getting Ideas From Recognited Personalities

Do you not believe you should adopt a minimalist lifestyle if the people listed below do?

The CEO of Apple, Steve Jobs, strongly supports minimalism. Apple products' success largely depends on their elegant, minimalist design and user-friendly interface, but Jobs elevated it even further. The main idea of his photography was to "simplify complexity." This method demonstrates that the focus is not on the complex product you sell but on how you contact customers and create lead generation strategies. He incorporated this into his lifestyle and applied it to his business.

People have reported little to no furniture in Jobs' home. He firmly believes in living a minimalist lifestyle.

Albert Einstein

Though he was a theoretical physicist, Albert Einstein is most known for his theory of relativity. But the documents also state that he lived a simple life and embraced minimalism. For Einstein, this meant he owned very little clothing, gave away most of his wealth, and cheek-surfed wherever he traveled. Despite everything, he continued to have fun occasionally, enjoying coffee, cigars, and music.

Michael Bloomberg

The former Mayor of New York City is extremely wealthy but owns less than six parcels of real estate. Although not much is known about Bloomberg's minimal expenditures, he appears to be giving away his wealth and cutting back on spending despite having extraordinarily large resources.

Gradually, Vincent Kartheiěr, the TV personality of Mad Men, began selling and giving away the items he no longer needed or desired. Surprisingly, Kartheiser had no teeth at all at one point. Even though he went to extremes, his frugal lifestyle is not typical of movie characters.

The Twilight Saga star Robert Pattinson may be well-known, but it seems he doesn't fit the typical lagging and spending type who shows no interest in owning things. The British musician, actor, and model may have frugal spending habits, yet he is actively involved in humanitarian efforts. He is a well-known supporter of numerous organizations and was the first ambassador for the GO Campaign in 2015.

Jane Siberry

Renowned Canadian singer and author Jane Siberry is a real minimalist who travels a lot. Carrying only two backpacks, a guitar, and a laptop, she travels back and forth, delivering her music. In addition, she doesn't exchange any money for her music on her website. It seems that Jane became weary of the harassment she received from her managers and ceased interacting with them. A few years later, she also sold the majority of her belongings. She currently has a single house and spends most of her time traveling.

Leonardo da Vinci

His favorite quote was, "Simplicity is the ultimate sophistication." According to his contemporaries, his character was friendly and attractive, and he was so kind that he fed all of his friends, regardless of their financial situation.

Chapter 3: The Secret to a Minimalist Lifestyle: Decluttering

We'll speak about specific ways you may start decluttering your life en route to a minimalist lifestyle now that you know the most crucial general actions you'll need to take to simplify your life and increase the joy and happiness you get from it. This is the real deal, and it will probably be the most difficult aspect of the lifestyle.

Stop the Flow

Before starting any sort of decluttering, think about plugging the "leak." You will be wasting your time and effort on pointless decluttering if you don't seal the leak that allows clutter to continuously enter your life. You will just replace every item you declutter with a new one.

Start by cutting back on your daily, weekly, and monthly purchases. Doing this will make it possible for your decluttering efforts to be successful.

Every Day, at Least One

As previously stated, getting rid of everything at once is unnecessary. I strongly advise focusing on only one junk item each day. Not only is it really simple to do, but imagine how much stuff, with constant practice, you could be able to let go of in just a year. Yes, precisely 365 items! You won't probably feel overwhelmed by the decluttering process if you just eliminate one item daily.

Begin Simply

Those who recently completed their first marathon will tell you they all began simply by running small distances. They also increased their running distance and speed as they grew stronger and more resilient, eventually completing a 42-kilometer marathon.

Living a simple lifestyle is a marathon, not a sprint, in a sense. Therefore, begin with the easiest things to let go of and then progressively get the strength and momentum to let go of the larger, more difficult-to-let-go-of items. In this manner, you'll be able to maintain your momentum and avoid feeling overtaken when switching to a minimalist lifestyle.

Make a Disposal Plan.

Although getting rid of items isn't difficult, it might not be as simple as you think it is if you have a lot of stuff, many of which you have some emotional links to. You'll need to plan your actions, just like you would with something worthwhile and reasonably difficult, like running your first full marathon. You're essentially planning for failure if you don't.

Examine all your alternatives for getting rid of stuff before you begin, such as selling, giving away, recycling, and donating. Decluttering and parting with your once-loved items will be easier and simpler if you research these options and determine which ones work best for particular objects. And what do you know? The more straightforward it gets, the more likely you'll stick to your plan and shift to a minimalist lifestyle!

Give Up the Obligation and Guilt Criteria

As part of your decluttering process, commit yourself to not using guilt or a sense of duty to guide your decisions when deciding what to keep or discard. The ability of an object to add significant value to your life is the only criterion by which you will decide whether or not to keep it in your collection. Let it go if it doesn't.

Disregard the Fear

The worry that you might need something again is one of the main justifications for holding onto items. Returning to the fundamental concept of needs is one of the best ways to undermine this rationale. First of all, necessities are items that you either can't live without or can live without, albeit not for very long or expensive. Second, being beneficial isn't the only requirement for a necessity. A thing could be helpful, but it's not always necessary to feel true happiness, fulfillment, significance, or survival. You may overcome the fear that prevents you from decluttering your life, office, and house by clearly defining what needs are on your prioritized list.

Nature Doesn't Always Give Material Gifts

Recall our discussion about preventing clutter from entering your life. That is by letting those around you know you would rather receive gifts of other kinds, such as experiences or quality time. If they are adamant about giving you something, then accept their money. Offer them material items that can complicate their lives if you don't tell them what you truly desire for a gift.

Maintain the Feel of Home in Your House

You shouldn't maintain your house like a hotel where visitors check in regularly. To be more precise, I'm saying that since you're not in the hospitality industry, you shouldn't overstock your house with items like silverware, linens, and pantry supplies. Just borrow extra items from your family or closest friends when you need to host guests for longer than a day. You may maintain your house clutter-free by simply returning the borrowed items after cleaning them once your guests have left.

Tips for the Uncommitted Minimalist: How to Live Simply

We are always yearning for more as our lives progress: more space, money, and time. What if you could use lessons to create more for your family and yourself by going in the opposite direction?

This is the fundamental precursor of the popular push towards minimalism. A lifestyle philosophy based on the understanding that anything unnecessary should be removed minimalism; rather than concentrating on "stuff" like tasks and assignments, minimalism aims for a simpler life.

Life can be difficult at times. Having a big house full of belongings is a labor-intensive, time-consuming job to maintain it all. The organizing and cleaning duties that accompany a high quality of life become a job unto themselves. It may be an exhilarating cycle.

A simpler lifestyle eliminates some of these stresses. The attraction of minimalism lies in its refusal to pursue the idea of "more."

But do you need to give up all of your desires to live a simpler lifestyle? Not always—minimumites would concur. The common misconception of minimalism is that to truly be free and happy, you must throw away all of your attachments. It's a lot easier to live frugally than that.

We are delving into the essence of minimalism today to demonstrate how simple it can be after you have established a personal approach to it. We'll review some simple ways to downsize your house and live more simply without resorting to drastic measures like extreme minimalism.

What Does Being a Minimalist Mean?

An individual who embodies the philosophy of minimalism is known as a minimalist. What, then, is minimalism? Minimalism originated as an artistic movement renowned for eliminating superfluous components to highlight essential features. Minimalism as a way of life photographs similarly. We are left with the things that matter most when we let go of the things that don't matter.

A MinimalizationAn Approach to House Organisation

It is a well-known fact that to make a new house or flat seem like home, you have to fill it with belongings. We make as many decorations and additions as possible to make the space feel welcoming.

Do you realize that you must organize and tidy everything you have more of? Not only does your environment need to be decluttered, but so does your mind and calendar. When you live a minimalist lifestyle, these items require less regular decluttering because you are already living simply. The concept of minimalism will make it easier for you to manage your time, keep your home cleaner, and ultimately live a simpler life.

Organising The House

I've prepared a list for you to use, but first, I want you to evaluate the area in your home. The likelihood is that it is crammed full of items. To evaluate the damage, you must proceed with the next step.

Step Six: Inventorying your possessions

Making a list of everything you own requires starting at the top of the house and working your way down. You probably thought your house was a beautiful space when you bought it. Over time, as your belongings increase, you may have come to believe that your home is modest; nevertheless, the reality is that having more stuff takes up much less space. After clearing your clutter, you'll have the extra room to appreciate and unwind. Using a pen and paper, take notes as you move from room to room, and include a list of the things that need to go. Keep in mind that shrinking furniture pieces is an additional option.

Which ornaments must be removed?

Which photos need removal?

Which add-ons must be removed?

Which curtains are out-of-date and darken the room?

Which furniture pieces must be replaced?

Which cabinets need further sorting in the space you have?

You should consider what you want to do with the stuff, and it will be helpful to have a location in your garage where you can temporarily store the extras. You can create spaces dedicated to:

Things that will be distributed

Things to be offered for sale during a garage sale

Those charitable items

Things that need to be disposed of

Recall that a piece of furniture that appears worn out to you can be just what a recently moved-in homeowner is searching for. It's not a waste. It all comes down to setting the proper priorities. You have the satisfaction of parting with things that no longer meet your needs and the wonderful sense of donating or selling something to someone for a fair price.

A few exceptions to the norm

You must understand that every home has issues. These could be located in the following house areas:

The laundry area

The Culinary

The pantry

The cabinets in the bathroom

The Wardrobe

These are places where a significant accumulation of stuff is kept in closets or cabinets, so they must be documented. You may need to dedicate more time to some areas as you declutter because there will be many moving objects and decision-making involved. When organizing your closet, for instance, you should be able to fit things you plan to sell, give as gifts, and discard that you no longer use. Try to examine each item individually and determine whether it makes you happier. It must be removed if it doesn't. Though you might worry that you won't have anything left to wear, the fun part about this practice is that you can wear less. All the stuff in your closet will fit you well and bring value to your life, and you can always add more items to match the ones you already own or enjoy.

There will be a ton of shabby underwear in your underwear drawer that you have washed and laundered till they no longer look their finest. You can even own brand-new underwear you never wear since it doesn't provide comfort for your body. Get rid of it. It's taking up space and complicating your life because you must search through the drawer each time you want new underpants. That is ineffective and doesn't improve your quality of life either.

You'll have random-purchase appliances in the kitchen that you seldom ever use. Get rid of them to make room for them. Don't allow anything to go bad in the freezer or the back of the refrigerator; instead, empty both and arrange your food so that labels are easily visible. It's better to have less. Your home will look more ordered and have less clutter, which will help you choose what you need rather than cause you to acquire unnecessary items.

You'll discover that you have expired medications in the bathroom. These should be disposed of at your pharmacy, as they have secure facilities for destroying medications. If you have unopened packs, you might be able to give them to your general practitioner so that others who cannot afford their medications can receive them. You'll also see that you own several cosmetic items you purchased with the hope that they would improve the quality of your skin or hair. Get rid of them if you are not using them. After a long day at work, the bathroom should be a sanctuary where you may rest and rejuvenate. Clear the clutter. Give yourself a fresh bathmat and towels, and put the old towels in the cleaning closet so they may be used for cleaning instead. A lovely plant with a pleasant scent would be a great addition, and the bathroom should smell clean and fresh. We frequently gather items in the bathroom that serve no purpose. It's time to part with those things now.

The washing room serves as a place for people to discard items. If so, ensure everything in the room is solely there to make your washday easier by going through everything. You certainly don't need all the old clothes that have been collecting dust at the bottom of the laundry basket for months. Get rid of them. If you have a place in this room where you can fold clothing straight out of the dryer, you can greatly streamline your washing process and save a ton of time because you won't have to iron them.

Every room in your house has to be cleared of clutter. You could be unsure of how to handle sentimental items. Why not give them now if these are items you wish to pass down through the family? Alternatively, you may package them and store them in the attic. Any workplace you see that is cluttered with items you know you need to move to make room for dust should be cleared out.

Examine the light that enters each chamber after you have completed your tour of them. Window treatments may make rooms appear smaller than they are. Dark drapes or curtains can be hung to block the light coming in through the window. If you want to declutter, swap bulky materials for gorgeously light linens. This will eliminate an always dusty area and let in natural light.

The Minimalist Worker, Chapter 5
There might be a lot of tension at work. There's a limit to how many deadlines and requests your boss or clients may make of you. Thankfully, there are actions you can do to lessen stress, workload, and time spent at work. One

such step is incorporating a minimalist lifestyle into your workflow and workstation. Here are a few easy pointers on how to go about it:

The Simplified Work Area

Your mind might be instantly cleared and motivated to work wisely when your desk is neat and well-organized. No matter how hectic a weekday becomes, it is ideal if your office is not exacerbating your tension.

Since a minimalist workspace only holds materials necessary for the user's job, each is unique to the user. But ideally, everything ought to be digital. Keeping everything on a laptop or desktop can free up much space and simplify file searching.

When designing a minimalist workstation, consider everything you need for work and everything you use daily. Next, ascertain how to make things as simple as possible. For example, the following components of a standard minimalist workspace:

A notebook. A laptop is great since it eliminates the need for additional cords and gadgets, making it space-efficient.

You should try to keep your office free of additional devices. Since emails are now the primary method of sending documents, some minimalists live without a printer, scanner, or fax machine.

Additionally, scanners are no longer necessary since objects and documents can now be delivered by email and photographed in good resolution. Data can also be sorted and scheduled using a computer. This will also remove the desk, chair, and a separate organizer requirement. Although most people would want to have these two fundamental items, it is acceptable if you choose to work while sitting on the floor. Since they have digital copies of all the required documents, most minimalists have a desk devoid of drawers. The desk would only be used for their computer and as an extra room if they needed to arrange the paper for a certain assignment. But most days, there's nothing on the desk.

A bookcase. To keep crucial papers and books orderly and out of the way during your busiest days, set aside a place for them if there are some objects you just can't part with.

To keep your minimalist office the way you like it, it is best to stop this collection from expanding in the future. For instance, you can buy electronic books rather than physical ones.

An inspiration source. In a minimalist workstation, bare walls and level surfaces are crucial since they leave the mind clear for new idea generation and help eliminate distractions. Naturally, this does not imply that your office has to be boring.

Placing one or two items that remind you of the original reason you are working so hard will help make it feel cozier. This might be a picture of your loved ones, an image of your objective, or a framed print of a phrase from your inspiration. Make this the main attraction in the space so that you can always look at it to get through difficult times.

The Work Flow of Minimalism

A workflow is the systematic procedure you use when allocating your working hours. The following processes would be included in your workflow if you were a writer: conceptualize, research, outline, draft, proofread, edit, and submit.

List all of the tools you'll need, digital and otherwise, under each phase. Next, devise a plan to streamline your workflow and arrange all the tools to make them conveniently accessible in one location, like a single bin, drawer, or folder. After that, get rid of or store the extraneous.

The following are some strategies for streamlining your workflow:

Maintain just one inbox. If you must maintain records, keep no more than one inbox tray on your desk to accommodate all your work-related documents, including notes. This will force you to go through your papers daily to avoid a pile-up and keep the remainder of your desk tidy.

Perform a daily "purge" of paperwork. Every day should conclude with the "inbox" empty to make room for fresh ones the next day. It is intended to be an inbox, not a storage container. Take one document at a time and go through the papers during the day. Make snap decisions and move quickly to complete chores by filing, discarding, or assigning them. You can also make a to-do list for tasks that can wait until later.

Keep your digital desktop organized. A minimalist's best friend is a tidy desktop, which allows you to focus on the most useful tools without being sidetracked by an excessive number of icons. Because it reduces visual stress, some minimalists even prefer having no icons on their desktops.

You can arrange all your icons into a single folder and designate it as "Temporary" if you also want a pristine desktop. Make two new folders inside this folder, one named "Active" and the other "Archive." Put your regularly used current documents and program shortcuts in the "Active" folder and the remaining files and documents in the "Archives" folder.

After that, get rid of every icon on your desktop. On a Mac, choose "Preferences," navigate to the "General" tab, and uncheck the box next to "Hard disks" under "Show these items on the Desktop." On a PC, right-click the desktop, select "View" from the menu, and uncheck the box next to "Show desktop icons."

After you've removed all of your icons, pick a peaceful desktop image with a minimalist theme or use it as your inspiration photo.

Establishing a simple workstation will greatly enhance your inventiveness and ingenuity. You will eventually come to view your workspace as a place where you may be productive and energized rather than a place where you must endure tension.

Lism Has The Power To Improve Your Life

Living a simpler existence free from the shackles of possessions and minimalism has many benefits beyond relieving stress. Though that is a huge plus, decluttering your home is about more than just not stabbing your toe when you try to urinate at three in the morning. Before deciding to go it alone and try living the lifestyle (which is, incidentally, highly encouraged), individuals are unaware of the various benefits of this concept that ingrains itself in opposition to Western consumerist ideas.

Less goods equals less debt, and debt reduction increases financial independence. After you pay off the credit card in full, stop using it. We're not advocating for you to give up on your education loans and sell everything you own; we're considering if you need that new, pricey jacket, you were ready to charge to your credit card. Even though your monthly credit card payment may only be $15, interest and credit card fees can quickly add up, turning that $100 jacket into a $150 one at the cost of not paying the full amount upfront.

Would you have paid the money in full if that was your only option? If yes, what is the initial reason for using the credit card? If not, you have spared not just the $100 you would have otherwise paid in interest and fees but also the additional $50 you would have lost.

Less stuff means more money to spend on the adventures you've always wanted to take part in, like kayaking in Yellowstone or traveling to Ireland.

You might even use that money to start saving for your own house. Nobody suggests that buying a house is a needless financial expenditure.

Adopting a minimalist mindset and way of living can also benefit the environment. You will have less to replace or discard if you own fewer items. Reducing the amount of possessions and "necessary stuff" we use can help lessen our environmental impact and maintain the health of our world. Constant consumerism is thought to be destroying the environment around us. Reduced product consumption produces less environmental pollution and fewer resources needed to produce the mounting things.

Time to be more productive also comes with this minimalist way of living. Less distracting and time-consuming items around you will allow you to focus more of your time and attention on important things. Eliminating consumerist distractions from your life can improve your quality of life because it replaces one source of attention with another, whether that be spending time with friends and family, going for a walk in your favorite spot, or working on that necessary task in a place that makes you smile. You can incorporate many activities that improve your current life into that extra time; for example, yoga, meditation, exercise, gardening, hiking, fishing, and hunting are all considered stress-relieving hobbies that many people just "do not have time for."

By giving away and eliminating items you eventually do not need, you can clear your mind of any distractions and free up time for these kinds of activities that can help you feel less stressed.

Furthermore, you may be confident that you lead by example for many people. If you are a parent, your kids will observe your behavior and take after you, modeling your way of living. If you detest how you spend money when you shop, but your children witness you doing it, they will develop the same spending habits as you and experience similar problems later in life.

However, if you can overcome those obstacles and live a less stressful life, you'll teach your kids that this is how life should be lived.

The same effect may impact friends, coworkers, and family members like your parents. In this book section, the adage "be the change you wish to see in the world" is extremely accurate, as modeling change for those around you is the most effective approach to affect change in others. Do it yourself rather than discuss it, consider whether to do it and then tell others it's a wonderful idea. Allow the transformation in your life to serve as the tangible evidence that others require to make the same shift in their lives.

Leading a simple lifestyle that replenishes your energy reserves is another wonderful benefit. Seeing the mess around them as they enter their houses reminds many that there are things they are letting go of. The mess may constantly remind us that we need to prioritize other areas of our lives above others or that we are perpetually behind on something. Furthermore, belongings have a strange ability to ingrain us in places we don't need to be.

Because we do not want to deal with the mess of clutter within our houses, having too much stuff can almost make it feel like a nuisance to apply for that new job and relocate to another state to take it.

We then use our belongings and clutter as the excuse for being unable to accept the job that would make us happier at this time, even though the income is a little less.

Your belongings are "rooting you down," so how much life are you missing out on?

When you have less of them, you are more inclined to move, travel, and discover places that might eventually lead to your happiness and to take those risks.

However, escaping the "comparison game" is one of the biggest advantages of leading a minimalist lifestyle. Our possessions are markers of our social standing, prosperity, and self-worth in modern society. Children are graded in middle school based on what they wear and whether or not it is a name brand. Teens are graded in high school according to the gadgets they own, including whether or not they have the newest iPhone model. Rating and comparing games persists in the adult world.

Recognize this: nobody will speak at your funeral one day about the amazing phone they had in high school or their amazing shoes in middle school. They will discuss who you were, how you lived, what principles you had or didn't have, and who you loved and didn't love. Nobody will ever recall the name of the designer of your wedding gown in the end. They are going to recall the kind of person you are. Can let go of the comparison and ranking game and enter a world where your value is determined by who you are and how you act rather than by what you own. This is because you won't need to stay updated with fashion or other trends. It will make room for the more general elements of the minimalist mindset to seep into every part of your life, and you will start to value what you already have rather than feeling envious of what you lack.

Why and How to Minimize Your Fitness and Eating Habits

Your minimalist lifestyle won't be complete until you incorporate healthy food and exercise routines. You're likely used to overindulging in food if you're not used to leading a simple existence. Regular exercisers are accustomed to working out hard and in excess rather than in moderation. This chapter addresses both of these harmful behaviors for you.

Making Eating Habits Simpler

Determining your body mass index (BMI) and the corresponding calories you need should be your priority. Two thousand four hundred calories a day is sufficient for adult males, and 2000 calories a day suits adult women. You should follow your healthcare provider's instructions if your body needs more because of a medical condition and your doctor says it's alright. But, you must suppress this urge if it has led you to routinely consume more calories than is recommended due to persistent cravings.

Breaking the bad habit of eating too often during the day is important. The sooner you break this eating pattern, the better for your health, as consuming large amounts of calories leads to obesity, which in turn causes diseases like diabetes, hypertension, and cardiovascular illnesses. You must, then, make your meal schedule as simple as possible.

Advice: Use this calculator to determine your daily caloric needs and how many calories you should consume.

Stay Away from Unhealthy Ingredients and Foods

Saying no to all the artificial additives and harmful meals is the next step towards streamlining your eating habits. Foods high in calories, cholesterol, trans fats, sodium, refined grains, high fructose corn syrup, and genetically engineered foods are included in this list. You can improve your productivity by eating foods free of these components, raising energy levels.

You also need to cut back on the various over-the-counter medications you consume. Doing this makes you less dependent on medications and allows your body to recover. This strengthens your immune system and reduces the medications your body needs.

Exercise and Fitness Plans That Are Minimalist

You must pay attention to your fitness and exercise regimens and how and what you eat. Excessive and insufficient exercise are detrimental to your health since they cause your body to become overexhausted and make you sluggish, boring, and obese. You must, therefore, choose the middle ground.

First, schedule some time each day for exercise. Engaging in moderate to intense exercise for thirty minutes three times a week is sufficient to maintain your health. If you are a bodybuilder and often engage in intense exercise, you should start exercising more moderately.

While doing a lot of exercise is beneficial, it takes too much time and complicates life. You get tense if you don't meet your exercise objectives in a single day. This demonstrates how your routine essentially saps your energy and prevents you from spending time with your loved ones or yourself. For this reason, you should make it more accommodating and simple for yourself so that it won't burden or worry you.

Getting Your Finances in Order

To live a well-rounded, minimalistic existence, you must apply minimalist strategies to your financial and money problems.

Reduce Your Expenditure Compared to Your Income

Determining how much money you make and spend each month is the first step towards budgeting and financial simplification. If your expenses exceed your income, you undoubtedly live a lavish lifestyle and overspending. You must alter your way of living even if your entire income equals your expenses.

Spend less than you earn to start. You must enumerate your fixed or absolute expenses and any additional ones to do that. Rent, utilities, food, medical costs, health insurance, and auto insurance (should you decide to purchase a car) should all be considered absolute expenses. You probably don't own a car if you're an "extreme" minimalist, in which case your car and petrol costs disappear. Even if you own a car, you should save it for emergencies only to save on car-related costs.

Anything above these are extra costs. Your expenses will immediately decrease if you reduce them. You can apply the 50-30-20 rule, which states that half of your income should go toward necessities (such as a mortgage, car, food, and other necessary expenses), thirty percent should go toward lifestyle choices (i.e., things you want but don't need), and twenty percent should go toward financial commitments (such as debt, retirement, etc.).

Refuse credit cards and obtain a sensible savings plan.

After that, you should say goodbye to every credit card in your wallet. They are a major drain on your budget and a contributor to your ongoing stress. Simply block them and discard them. Rather, you ought to obtain a sensible savings plan with a moderate rate of return. When things go rough, this will help you get by.

Use these techniques to attain minimalism in your financial dealings.

Chapter 5: Cutting Down on Your Connections

"Edit your life with ruthlessness and frequency." After all, it's your masterpiece. Nathan W. Morris

With minimalism, your relationships can become more meaningful, joyful, and less tense and miserable. Here, minimalism entails forming bonds with people you genuinely appreciate and limiting your social interactions to those who are significant and upbeat.

Let's examine how you might apply minimalism to this area of your life.

Examine Your Various Relationships In Your Life

Consider your relationships—friends, family, and relatives—and consider how important each one is to you in life. Which of your relationships are a burden, and which are genuinely vital to you?

If a friend consistently brings you down, but finds it impossible to cut ties with them because they support you monetarily when you need it, consider if you truly want to be friends with them. You won't need his or her assistance, and you won't have to put up with all of the jabs they hurl at you if you stop buying pointless items and start saving.

Analyze every relationship that is important to you but that you haven't been spending enough time on lately. Do you make sacrifices when it comes to family time? Do you make your kids feel forgotten by not spending much time with them during the week? If so, it's time to rearrange your priorities and give your full attention to everyone who truly matters to you.

Make more time for all the positive, caring, and encouraging individuals in your life, and gradually remove yourself from everyone who doesn't mean much to you or who depresses you.

Spend Time with Loved Ones Without a Phone

Make more time for your loved ones after reevaluating your relationships and determining which ones to preserve and which to let go of. Ensure you don't use any electronics, phones, or social media during your time with them. Spend some genuine, quality time with your children instead of using your phone while watching a movie with friends or while you're sitting with them. If you sit beside your spouse, pay attention to what she has to say and share your tales and experiences with her. You have a deeper understanding of your loved ones and begin to appreciate their presence when you genuinely start chatting and listening to them. This enables you to find fulfillment in them rather than in devices and toys, which rarely make you feel content or at ease.

Talk about minimalism with your loved ones.

Talk to your loved ones about implementing minimalism in your life. Inform your family that you'll start living a simpler lifestyle and appreciate it if they do the same. Set a good example by doing it yourself before imposing it on others. Your children will be motivated to adopt a simpler lifestyle when they witness your content with fewer clothes, electronics, and possessions.

It will be simpler for you to maintain minimalism, and you will always be content if your loved ones do as well. Reduce the amount of stuff in your life by gradually simplifying your finances and career. You can learn how to accomplish it in the next chapter.

Chapter Four: Environment

It may surprise you to hear, but receiving an arrangement of flowers typically makes you feel happy. This is a result of you incorporating nature within your house. Similarly, your home's outdoor area can enhance the enjoyment you get from being there. Consider adding a sitting area directly outside your French doors if they go to the backyard. This will increase your living space and allow family members to stretch out a bit. It's amazing how nature can bring the outside in. Consider getting plants that are visible from the inside but live outside.

You likely don't get enough of nature if you live in a town. In addition to adding smells and air to your home, plants are a highly healthful addition. They can also give the impression that your house is a more laid-back place. But don't go overboard. A lovely orchid in the bathroom can serve as the room's focal point and an aromatherapy addition. A single bonsai positioned prominently gives a space more depth. Isn't a single focus point preferable to a whole stack of crammed shelves full of junk?

Make the most of your living space by utilizing color, but remember that a lovely arrangement of flowers looks nicer on kitchen worktops than a large collection of inactive gadgets. Clear the area, but ensure that anything you add gives your house a unique touch. Even though this chapter is brief, it is nonetheless essential. This goal is to show that you can have a fashionable and inviting design for your home without breaking the bank. Simplify everything and include items that bring you joy. Typically, flowers and plants do.

Dividend tip number six: Throw away broken pieces

This is a straightforward tip that goes without saying. I wrote this tip for the handymen and handywomen who can fix broken items around the house but never get around to doing it.

I am unable to relate to it. I'm a very handy person. However, I've seen how some people who use this incredible talent to improve things behave.

that's akin to saying, "Oh, I can't throw it out because I know I can fix it." Meanwhile, your shattered bonds continue to pile up.

Be honest with yourself. Rather than putting these projects in your "I'll do it later" pile, consider how life has been without them. If it was indeed that little, you would have likely fixed it by now.

Therefore, let go of the past and mourn the broken things in your life, then move on. If you have trouble throwing it out, take it to the tip. The parts might be used by someone else for something they are creating. It might just be the puzzle's missing piece.

Dictator tip number 7: Give books and magazines to hotel emergency rooms.

Have you ever visited a hospital emergency room? Unfortunately, I have spent a fair amount of time in these rooms.

The selection of reading material is typically made five or more years in advance. A few more pertinent reading materials would have been nice while waiting in an emergency room. Or at least a little more variety!

Divider tip number eight: Roll your thirties.

Declutingting does not always require you to be aware of your boundaries. Sometimes, all you need to do is rearrange an area to create more mental and physical space.

A great example of this may be seen in your closet, particularly in your t-shirts and tank tops.

Declutter tip number nine: Reduce your towel rotation

I used to own five tokens. I'm not sure why. I guess that's what my mother got me.

However, I've happily lived with just two earrings in my repertoire since becoming a minimalist. That way, I have an ice pack to use while my tatters are drying in case I need to wash them.

I am not sure why I would require more than two. Ladies may contend that they require an additional towel to dry their hair. You can declutter if you have more than three teeth (including one for the beach).

The best thing about this tip is that your divorced teeth can be useful in other situations. To start with, you may use them as rags to use around the house.

Dividend Tip Number 10: Organize before making a purchase.

Before rushing out and purchasing numerous storage boxes and organizers to aid in decluttering, give yourself some time to organize first.

You may realize through the organization procedures that you don't require any additional storage facilities.

I believe that sometimes, we become excited about what our surroundings will seem like once we've moved on.

Decluttering does not involve design. It has to do with living consciously. Treat yourself to a trip to Kiki K just after you've completed the difficult work.

Trickle down to number eleven: Be truthful in your vision.

Continuing from the last tip, try to be realistic about your vision. Comparing yourself to gorgeous minimalist homes on social media and home décor magazines is simple.

I have it. Minimalism is currently a seductive topic. Naturally, it's acceptable to desire an aesthetically pleasing home.

All you have to do is set reasonable expectations for yourself.

Your home's appearance could differ depending on how it was constructed, including the materials used for the flooring and the color of the walls.

Declutter tip number twelve: The four-box method

The four-box method is a fantastic decluttering technique I have tried and tested.

The idea is to have four boxes, each serving a different purpose:

● A box used for discarding items ● A box used for storing items ● A box used for donating items

● A box stores items, though your goal is to reduce. Some items may be essential but not necessary for day-to-day living. A prime example of this would be Christmas decorations or antique photo albums with sentimental value.

Trick Number 13: Create a spot for incoming papers. Papers frequently account for a significant portion of our content. We placed them in various locations: the countertop, table, desk, drawer, top of our dresser, and inside our car. We were unable to locate anything at all! Set up an inbox display or ĕpot in your home (or office, for that matter) and keep papers stacked somewhere other than that spot. AVAILABLE MAIL? Place it in the email. Have you received your school papers?

Place it in the email. Receipts, guarantees, manuals, notifications, flyers? Within the inbox! Your paper can be transformed by making this one small adjustment.

Number 14 Decluter tip: Scan your paperwork

After completing tip 13, you could go one step further and choose a 100% paperless workflow. If your system is configured properly, you can easily import important documents using your smartphone, store them on your computer or in the cloud, and then retrieve all physical documents.

This is the way we handle our paperwork.

Divider tip number 15: Organize by categories rather than rooms

Time is one of the biggest obstacles to decreasing. Furthermore, it is entirely unquestionable.

For this reason, it is best to break the project down into smaller parts.

Typical decluttering advice will advise you to concentrate on one room at a time. But, based on the room, there's a chance you won't finish the task in the allotted time. This level of deception can completely dissuade you from trying again.

A different method to apply decluttering is to concentrate on categories rather than rooms.

Therefore, instead of concentrating on the kitchen, aim to clear the drawers.

Instead of concentrating on clearing your bed linen, concentrate on clearing just your towels.

Dealing with categories allows you to achieve quick wins. Moreover, it brings similar items together, simplifying whether to keep, donate, store, or discard (see tip 12).

Chapter 6: Step 4-Refuse Needless Items

Say no to everything freely offered to you and make a conscious effort to say no to your growing desires as you work on getting rid of unnecessary items and, as a result, a lot of stress from your life. This is a crucial step because you can never truly practice minimalism if you keep adding more items to your home. Here's how to implement this significant change in your life gradually.

How To Turn Down Free Things

There can be instances where someone offers you free items. Maybe your mom bought two fruit bowls and wants you to have one, or you went to a presentation where they gave you free caps. You add clutter to your life if you take any of those items when you don't need them. Say no to free things if you want to live a modest lifestyle. Saying no thank you respectfully to someone who offers you something is appropriate, even if it is free and you know you don't need it. Accept it and give it away as soon as you are alone yourself if refusing that thing will harm that person's feelings.

If you get a lot of gifts for your birthday, give away and donate all the extras and replacements. If you want to keep anything given to you for free, find out what alternatives you have and discard one. If the blanket you have at home is in poor condition and you received one, throw it away.

Quickly assess whether you need anything before taking it or are just hoarding more stuff. If you only want more stuff, get rid of the object as soon as possible.

To ensure that you only keep what you truly need, practice saying no to temptations and wants and accepting freebies.

How to Refuse Yourself

Go over the description of the life you want to materialize every morning when you get up and use it as motivation to not accumulate more possessions than you need.

As you finish your daily duties, be attentive to your temptations and stay aware of them throughout the day. Give everything you do your all. This increases your awareness of your task and the random ideas and urges that arise.

Before making a purchase, consider whether you need the item. Is that new clothing really what you need, or is it just a passing fancy you can ignore? Also, avoid purchasing additional items for the same purpose if you own fulfilling items.

When you feel yourself losing the fight against temptation, take a few deep breaths and get out of the scenario that makes you want to give in to your wants. If you are in a mall and desperate to buy a new phone that you do not need, get out of there quickly. You'll probably have forgotten about that temptation by the time you get home if you head straight home and nowhere else.

Focus on what you have and what makes your life more meaningful to divert your attention. When you feel like something is lacking in your life or are tempted to make an unnecessary purchase, review the list of things you must be grateful for.

It will get easier to resist temptation if you follow these suggestions regularly.

Chapter 4: The Minimalist Approach to Developing Confidence

You can lack confidence if you have been ingrained in the consumption society of your community. Maybe you were buying into the idea because you thought it would boost your self-esteem. But when your home has been transformed, I would advise you to start meditation if you truly want to boost your confidence. This is due to several factors. One is that you get more at ease with your identity; the other is that, as I've previously mentioned, you learn to breathe correctly. There are two ways that this boosts your self-esteem. Your new home and way of life will make you proud to host guests, and your meditation practice will give you more self-assurance in your mental abilities. You will learn how to meditate if you decide to take yoga lessons, but first, I'll give you a quick rundown of what this entails so you can plan to perform one meditation session every day.

You do it daily because it helps you train your mind to see things more simply.

Your patience increases as you practice meditation daily. When you live a minimalist lifestyle, you no longer need to defend your possessions or lack thereof since you are confident in your judgment. Regular practice facilitates the peaceful condition of acceptance, and once you're there, you'll discover that you've also found peace with who you are. It took me some time to grasp the benefits of meditation when I first started doing it many years ago. Still, the breathing techniques and the meditation helped me feel refreshed and gave me a renewed sense of purpose for my life, even if I had felt like I didn't measure up in the past.

Because meditation fosters a certain level of self-acceptance, it also aids in self-confidence building. You experience a balance, unlike anything you may find in the modern world. The process becomes simpler when you begin to assess yourself by who you know yourself to be rather than by what other people think of you. There isn't much more you can do to alter who you are if you are already the finest version of yourself. On the other hand, meditation will provide you with many suggestions for further developing your spirituality and improving yourself.

I had no idea how much adopting a minimalist lifestyle would impact every aspect of my life. While my life seems relatively simple to them, some who laughed at the concept are now wishing they had followed the same path since they are still burdened with material possessions and mental pain. It helps that I no longer worry about the little things. You'll always feel inadequate if you're the type of person who gets anxious in social situations. Working toward minimalist objectives makes you stop caring about what other people think of you, and the confidence you have as a result is incredible. For instance, I never would have had the confidence to speak about the minimalist lifestyle in front of a large group of people. Still, now that I know that living a minimalist lifestyle may benefit many people, I can do it.

I once asked someone if they would save anything in a house fire. Though it was merely a hypothetical question, the response was obvious. The man promised to keep his instrument. To him, it held greater significance than anything else he owned. You'll also be surprised at how little many of your belongings mean to you when you ask yourself this question. In this instance, the individual considered adopting a minimalist lifestyle, which he has already done successfully. His guitar is the only item he keeps on display and holds in high regard in his world; the stark white walls contrast sharply with this. This is his family room.

He used to have a hard time finding time for music because he needed to do so many other things. He has gained newfound confidence as a result of simplifying his life, and he can now play the guitar whenever he wants to without worrying about upsetting the house's other residents. Every household member decides on priorities and is happy they did, as the house serves as a hub for unity and provides them with a lifestyle they never would have imagined feasible.

In a way, having less material belongings prevents obstacles from standing in the way of goals. As for me, I can speak to being content with my life and capable of carrying on a meaningful conversation, even though that would not have been the case a few years ago. You can accomplish so much more when your home and thoughts are decluttered. My work has transformed to the point that it consists of things I would have only fantasized about in the past but never truly recognized as real possibilities.

Because yoga makes me more graceful and causes my body to respond in a manner it never has, it has also increased my confidence. I don't always feel sick. Even the smallest ache or suffering doesn't bother me; instead, I use my intellect to process it and determine whether it's self-inflicted or genuine.

Sustaining Optimal Health

Living well enables you to make the most of every day. That state of affairs isn't assured, though. It must be approached as a goal.

For years, schools have taught students how to lead healthy lives. Still, a lot of people engage in unhealthy behaviors. Consequently, they experience ailments linked to their lifestyle. Alcohol consumption (3.3 million deaths), excessive salt intake (4.1 million deaths), tobacco use (7.2 million deaths), and inadequate physical exercise (1.6 million deaths) are responsible for millions of deaths. Too many lives were lost as a result of changeable behavior.

Minimalism opposes these kinds of harmful behaviors. Alcohol and tobacco cause clutter in the body. They ought to be avoided as a result. Salt doesn't have to be eliminated from your diet; make sure you only use modest amounts of it. You can find more time for exercising if you spend less time playing, watching, or browsing. Committing to self-care is the first step.

The Worth of Health

You must invest time and work into maintaining your fitness if you are committed to your health. Plan your meals and workouts. Additionally, you ought to acquire enough sleep. These aren't particularly novel suggestions. However, it can be challenging to maintain good behavior when so many temptations are available. You should also learn to resist those temptations to stay healthy; junk food is the most popular.

Getting Rid of Junk Food

Nutrient-poor foods and beverages are referred to as junk food. You get a full feeling from it. You no longer feel the urge to eat the more nutrient-dense varieties. Junk food is a bad choice because it raises the risk of several illnesses. Such meals can exacerbate the symptoms and signs of an existing sickness.

Regretfully, a lot of junk food is produced by large organizations. They portray their products as safe and even healthy because of their intensive marketing.

You already know that alcohol, chips, and candy are bad for you. However, did you realize that not all purported substitutes are that nutrient-dense?

Fruit juices are frequently promoted as healthful alternatives to soft drinks, energy drinks, and beverages with artificial sweeteners. They are just as horrible as the latter due to their sugar content. To be fair, occasionally consuming natural juice has health advantages. However, daily usage is excessive.

Although milk and coffee are widely considered acceptable beverages, they are nevertheless not healthful. Milk, indeed, helps build strong bones. However, it can make you more susceptible to skin disorders like acne.

One to three cups of coffee daily, used in moderation, might not have any negative effects. It might even offer advantages like improved mental clarity and a decreased chance of depression. If you drink more than three glasses each day, you may be increasing your risk of developing a cardiac issue. Overindulgence also hurts your mood and quality of sleep.

The healthiest beverage is still water. You don't have to purchase any further beverages. Quinoa and cashew milk are good substitutes for fresh milk if you miss the real thing.

Another item you want to stay away from is processed beef. This includes corned beef, ham, hotdogs, sausage, and beef jerky. This kind of cuisine is linked in many studies to heart disease and cancer.

Getting Ready for Meals

The good news is that various healthful eating options are still available. They can rival or surpass their harmful counterparts in terms of flavor.

Vegetables and fruits are included in the group of healthful foods. Purchase fresh produce from farmer's markets whenever possible. You can visit your neighborhood grocery store if it isn't a practical choice. Make sure you only eat in-season; it is less likely to be imported fruits and vegetables.

Making your food is a good idea because it's usually less expensive. Additionally, you may be more certain that your meal doesn't contain unhealthy ingredients.

Not everyone is a talented chef. Thankfully, if you put in the effort, you can learn how to do it. If you're not good in the kitchen, you can still enjoy various raw fruits and veggies. Choose raw nuts and fruits over ice cream and chips.

Brussels sprouts, broccoli, kale, and lettuce are veggies you can eat raw or cooked. To make them more delicious, you can even add dressing. Consider experimenting with root crops such as celery root, parsnips, and beets.

However, there are several veggies that you should never eat uncooked. They consist of wild mushrooms, potatoes, eggplants, and kidney beans. Raw spinach, asparagus, and tomatoes are edible. It will be preferable to cook them if you wish to reap additional health benefits.

They can be used to produce green salads or vegetable salads. Alternatively, you might roast some of the vegetables. You can eat eggs and seafood to meet your other dietary needs. They can also be used as meat substitutes. Tofu is yet another excellent option. It's generally tasteless, although it takes flavors well. Occasionally, you may also turn to chicken-based meals.

Simply put, preparing different meals at every mealtime is not feasible. You might feel inclined to stockpile time-saving kitchen appliances if that's your goal. Make your meals in batches rather than preparing them three times a day. It can be completed in the evening. You can prepare everything that has to be peeled, chopped, diced, or marinated in the morning.

Additionally, make your dressings. Olive oil is a wise choice because it can be used as a salad dressing. You should save salt, pepper, vinegar (apple cider or balsamic), and honey for your homemade dressings.

Chapter 5: Emphasize the value above the status

The status issue is that, in the end, it is determined by other people. Ultimately, it becomes a common story accepted by consensus among others.

Regretfully, it depends on the erratic nature of human nature. People can alter their thoughts. Thus, you do not influence them. It happens that people abandon those they once exalted to the skies.

This keeps happening over and over. Why shouldn't you experience it? Why do you stand out from the crowd? You give yourself so much power when you realize that value, not prestige, matters most. You break away from the belief that value is correlated with price.

Let's be honest: many people believe that their expensive clothing makes them appear valuable. People believe they have something in life because of the high value of the car they drive. You are free when you let go of the idea that price must determine value. As a result, you find enjoyment in the possessions you have acquired. You quit thinking of yourself in such demeaning terms and adopt a more realistic perspective on life.

If everything about you—what you wear, the cars you drive, the zip codes you reside in, the size of your house—is just a collection of numbers that signify different things to other people. If that were all there were to define who you are, you would be reduced to price signals. You will be this little, helpless, inconsequential person addicted to the admiration of others all the time.

That regard is erratic. That external social approbation can go in an instant. When that happens, what will you do? Then, what worth do you have?

Who will love you if you don't love yourself? Loving yourself via other people is the worst kind of self-love. They are not stand-ins for you. Why should they give a damn about you when they have enough trouble trying to love themselves?

Concentrate on embracing and accepting who you are. It is not the solution to compare the value of the items you purchase to their price. Instead, pay more attention to function than brand recognition. Consider a product's functionality over brand loyalty before making a purchase. Does it do the task or not? Does it have enough durability? When it comes to true self-esteem, you make a significant advancement if you concentrate on this rather than brand reputation.

Contrast this with the usual scenario where a consumer purchases goods based on a brand's reputation. They would say, "Okay," after choosing one of two items. Many more people respect this brand. If I purchase this brand, many people will like, envy, or respect me. However, a small number of individuals are aware of that brand. How can I benefit from it?

Consider the function as an alternative to doing that analysis. Does it maintain a dry and warm foot? Is its duration long? Do you think it looks decent, personally? Is it going to hold its form for a long time? These are the items that need your attention. Prioritize functionality over symbolism or brand reputation.

Pay attention to efficacy as well. Consider this while purchasing a car: How long would it last? In the long run, what type of headaches can you anticipate from it? Consider these concepts rather than status. "Does this convey that I am a very successful person or part of this elite neighborhoodthat I live in?" is not a thought that you should be having.

You need to realize that, in the end, you're paying more for something you can't control besides the status. You're in charge of signals that rely on other individuals. How meaningless is that?

Take the long route.

You must be patient if you truly want to overcome the belief that high worth equals great prestige and that price is a good indicator of both. Put otherwise, consider the overall worth of use.

In other words, if you purchased two goods, one for $100 and the other for $1,000, you might conclude that one is too pricey while the other is a no-brainer as it is less expensive. The more expensive item's total usage value, calculated on a per-user basis, would be precisely $1 if it could be used a thousand times. However, the less expensive item only had two uses, meaning that its precise cost or value per use was $50.

It should be clear from this angle that the $1,000 item is the superior deal. Consider the worth of the entire use rather than just the status symbol. I am not referring to luxury value here. Because the $1,000 item is $1,000, it has much to recommend from a pure luxury standpoint.

Although it has an upscale price point, you must go above and beyond. Consider total use value instead. You relieve yourself of the need to buy new things continually by doing this.

Purchase fewer items. Pay attention to how it is used and the real value it provides. To further this, consider purchasing fewer items by considering their numerous uses. Put another way, invest in items that serve a variety of purposes. In this method, you make fewer purchases altogether.

Make an effort to break free from your addiction to material possessions, as this addiction is ultimately founded on the flawed and debilitating notion that value is inextricably linked to status and cost.

How A Minimalist Lifestyle Can Improve Your Quality Of Life

Living a simpler existence free from the shackles of possessions and minimalism has many benefits beyond relieving stress. Though that is a huge plus, decluttering your home is about more than just not stabbing your toe when you try to urinate at three in the morning.

Less goods equals less debt, and debt reduction increases financial independence. After you pay off the credit card in full, stop using it. We're not advocating for you to give up on your education loans and sell everything you own; we're considering that you were ready to charge to your credit card if you need that new, pricey jacket. Even though your monthly credit card payment may only be $15, interest and credit card fees can quickly add up, turning that $100 jacket into a $150 one at the cost of not paying the full amount upfront.

Would you have paid the money in full if that was your only option? If yes, what is the initial reason for using the credit card? If not, you have spared not just the $100 you would have otherwise paid in interest and fees but also the additional $50 you would have lost.

Less stuff means more money to spend on the adventures you've always wanted to take part in, like kayaking in Yellowstone or traveling to Ireland.

You might even use that money to start saving for your own house. Nobody suggests that buying a house is a needless financial expenditure.

Adopting a minimalist mindset and way of living can also benefit the environment. You will have less to replace or discard if you own fewer items. Reducing the amount of possessions and "necessary stuff" we use can help lessen our environmental impact and maintain the health of our world. Constant consumerism is thought to be destroying the environment around us. Reduced product consumption produces less environmental pollution and fewer resources needed to produce the mounting things.

Time to be more productive also comes with this minimalist way of living. Less distracting and time-consuming items around you will allow you to focus more of your time and attention on important things. Eliminating consumerist distractions from your life can improve your quality of life because it replaces one source of attention with another, whether that be spending time with friends and family, going for a walk in your favorite spot, or working on that necessary task in a place that makes you smile. You can incorporate many activities that improve your current life into that extra time; for example, yoga, meditation, exercise, gardening, hiking, fishing, and hunting are all considered stress-relieving hobbies that many people just "do not have time for."

By giving away and eliminating items you eventually do not need, you can clear your mind of any distractions and free up time for these kinds of activities that can help you feel less stressed.

Furthermore, you may be confident that you lead by example for many people. If you are a parent, your kids will observe your behavior and take after you, modeling your way of living. If you detest how you spend money when you shop, but your children witness you doing it, they will develop the same spending habits as you and experience similar problems later in life.

However, if you can overcome those obstacles and live a less stressful life, you'll teach your kids that this is how life should be lived.

The same effect may impact friends, coworkers, and family members like your parents. In this book section, the adage "be the change you wish to see in the world" is extremely accurate, as modeling change for those around you is the most effective approach to affect change in others. Do it yourself rather than discuss it, consider whether to do it and then tell others it's a wonderful idea. Allow the transformation in your life to serve as the tangible evidence that others require to make the same shift in their lives.

Leading a simple lifestyle that replenishes your energy reserves is another wonderful benefit. Seeing the mess around them as they enter their houses reminds many that there are things they are letting go of. The mess may constantly remind us that we need to prioritize other areas of our lives above others or that we are perpetually behind on something. Furthermore, belongings have a strange ability to ingrain us in places we don't need to be. Because we do not want to deal with the mess of clutter within our houses, having too much stuff can almost make it feel like a nuisance to apply for that new job and relocate to another state to take it.

We then use our belongings and clutter as the excuse for being unable to accept the job that would make us happier at this time, even though the income is a little less.

Your belongings are "rooting you down," so how much life are you missing out on?

When you have less of them, you are more inclined to move, travel, and discover places that might eventually lead to your happiness and to take those risks.

However, escaping the "comparison game" is one of the biggest advantages of leading a minimalist lifestyle. Our possessions are markers of our social standing, prosperity, and self-worth in modern society. Children are graded in middle school based on what they wear and whether or not it is a name brand. Teens are graded in high school according to the gadgets they own, including whether or not they have the newest iPhone model. Rating and comparing games persists in the adult world.

www.ingramcontent.com/pod-product-compliance
Lightning Source LLC
Chambersburg PA
CBHW050202130526
44591CB00034B/1835